Midwest Gothic

D1565209

MIDWEST GOTHIC

poems

Laura Donnelly

Winner of the Richard Snyder Memorial Prize

The Ashland Poetry Press

Copyright © 2020 by Laura Donnelly

All rights reserved. Except for brief quotations in critical reviews, this book, or parts thereof, must not be reproduced in any form without permission of the publisher. For further information, contact the Ashland Poetry Press, Ashland University, Ashland, OH 44805, www.ashlandpoetrypress.com.

Printed in the United States of America
ISBN: 978-0-912592-88-6
Library of Congress Card Catalogue Number: 2019953780

Cover art: Debora Greger, "After Eden, Eve, I," courtesy of Abbott and Holder Gallery, London.
Cover design: Nicholas Fedorchak
Author photo: Veronica Gray

Acknowledgements

Grateful acknowledgement is made to the following publications in which poems from this book previously appeared, sometimes in earlier format or with different titles.

Apercus Quarterly: "Theme and Variations"
The Baltimore Review: "Birding"
Columbia Poetry Review: "*Rheum rhabarbarum* (Rhubarb)"
Compose: "Miss Missaukee, 1966"
DMQ Review: "Summer"
Freshwater Review: "Alice at Five Years Old" and "Inheritance"
Grist: "This Other Music"
Harpur Palate: "Not Yours"
Harvard Review: "Boat Song in F-sharp Minor"
Jet Fuel Review: "The Jack Loom," "After Blake," and "Garden Vernacular"
Indiana Review: "Eden through Milk Eyes"
Midwestern Gothic: "Homestead Triptych"
Mississippi Review: "The Perimeter"
Missouri Review: "Of Knowledge"
PANK: "Midwest Gothic"
Passages North: "*Jardin sous la pluie*" and "Exodus"
Poets.org: "The Carolina Wren"
Psaltery & Lyre: "Doxology"
Sweet: "An Ordinary Sleep"
Stone Canoe: "Elsie and Florence" and "The Last Supper"

For Karen Alice Donnelly

and in memory of
Angeline Quist (1923–2012)
Alice Slachter (1901–1989)

Contents

IV

Who saved it?—
Women
of good wild stock

—Lorine Niedecker, "Wintergreen Ridge"

I

Midwest Gothic

i.

I am taking the terrible, blistered mirror,
casting over empty oil lamps
and their globes.

Through long-shadowed halls over
pine boards creaking, cracked attic stairs,
I will gather you back.
                              Tear off the sheets—

The dollhouse has only three walls but the pond
is small enough to drown a child.

Tell me the worst winter.

Burnt-wet boards adrift. Blue marbles spilling
across the long porch,
a clatter of cat eyes in glass.

ii.

The rain made us admit our sadness
as if it weren't already worn like a headlamp.

You need *something* to say
            over dinner.
                        I keep saying *rain*
when I mean has the nest
been abandoned?

Have your legs longed to swim

in the icy pool?
                    I keep saying
when all I mean is rain
and the rain and yes
and more rain.

iii.

The lilac branch cracked in the storm so my mother
tied it back with old nylons. The basement
flooded so she sat on the stoop
with a spoon. This duct tape
keeps the radio working, but you can't
change the station, the decades we spent
at that frequency. In the middle
of the night, she rose to make bread,
punching it down in a veil of yeast
over the stove. She crocheted
a blanket but it grew too long and she never
turned the row, so really, it was a rope.
Ariadne wracked her brain for some maze
to crack, saying *take this, take this*—
find your way back.

Charlotte Sometimes

The book disappeared
like Charlotte disappeared,
unfinished, another one
taking its place.

Recalled, twenty-five years
into the future—a boarding house,
new girl, how she travelled
back in time and awoke
someone else—*Clare,*
but no clarity who she was.

I pictured white dresses
despite described uniforms
moving flat-footed down rows
of dorm beds. No parents—

and whether she made it back
to her own time, I don't know.
I did. The white eyelet dress
a figment, one of the first
fictions left behind.

Elsie and Florence

*Our cows ran loose, no fences, and towards evening we had to look
for them and fetch them home. They had bells on to help find them.
My sister and I would walk along the log roads and pretend we were
other people, I was Elsie and she was Florence.*
 —Alice Slachter

Evening new on our shoulders, the bells
are a copper we anticipate, unfenced.
We turn, or don't turn, and what we know
of the body's tendency to imagine itself
another body, we can't say. Or rather,
to say *I sleep your same sleep
every night*, a blanket
hung across the middle of the room,
our parents on the other side. To say
Sister. In the woods, there was a playhouse
and those cracked dishes for ornament. *Come home,
come home* it calls as we walk farther.
Then a chorus of bells like rusty hands
clapping us into dusk.

Alice at Five Years Old

In the photo, she sits
on the right-hand side
of the wagon, her sister beside her.
The rest of the children stand
like a row of fence posts
ending at their parents.

Their dirt-creased family
has clearly been posed
or posed themselves to show
a wagon, a small house, a barn.

Someday, when the girl meets
her mother-in-law,
they'll share a bowl of oatmeal
as if it's the body of Christ.

Later still, she'll offer
two tablets of saccharine
for my tea
before taking her leave.

Hear us, oh Lord, in our longest day's
shadow of bones—

the delphinium grows
from her body
in a choir of indigo.

Homestead Triptych

i. White Pines

This is the second growth in even rows.
This, the between.

Today we're hip high, but in eighty years
our limbs will loom over you,

taller than steeples spurring the sky.
The idea was a windbreak,

but see how we leave our shadows
in the eaves, our sticky-sweet scent

on your clothes?

ii. Cemetery

Because infant deaths. Because a small
hillside. Because the birds, this morning,

and I name so few,
how I've failed you.

Because you sleep in another
century, and sisters with names like

Hattie and *Ginny* born
and buried one hundred yards apart

but on either side we're accelerating
particles. We recall the cramped ship,

will our ashes to float without mark.

iii. Homestead

Grandmother rocked her sister until grooves formed
in the floor like twin spines. At eighty-eight,

it's her favorite to tell. And the drive
to California (though not the drive back).

Dort was my baby, she sighs.
Wrapped in colicky nights, the pines

barely begun but already that shhh
of rough silk, the room empty but

for their back-again-forward
remembering a creak in the dark.

Primula vulgaris (Primrose)

Add compost, manure,
the pulverized feathers of chickens condensed
into bags with names like *Flower Tone,*
Holly Tone, some that come right out,
say *Blood Meal.*

Grandmother does not want to leave
her house for the nursing home.
Mother does not want to leave
her house for the divorce.

Fist size and still green
against November's frost,
each plant's roots are briefly exposed.
Our favorites bloom fuchsia
with yellow centers, wild as cats' eyes
and bright as slits of flame.

Blood and bone, I prepare earth,
separate and transplant the primrose.
In the dreams, I grind feathers
and spade their powdery remains
into still warm soil.

Stachys byzantina (Lamb's Ear)

Mother says let the seeds
fall where they may.
Aunt says pinch between
thumb and pointer. Lamb of God,

what happens to your soft ears
when winter takes its bride?
What moon tucks in this frosty tide?
I clench my teeth without thinking

and rain turns into ice. October,
November, the ends
crinkle against my fingers
and the old diary won't suffice.

Lamb of God, when does water
ever turn into wine?
When does it turn into blood?
And what about what is mine?

Inheritance

Angie had diphtheria
and forever her mother's hand
checking her forehead,
calling her in from the fields.
They let her attend school
instead of canning tomatoes.
I have her rhubarb and her love
of reading at night.

Alice raised six children
in a coop they called *the shanty*.
She sent them
to neighbors with buckets
for water, the pump handle
wailing across the dirt road.
I have her brown hair,
imagine it dunked in a tub
by the stove to wash
when the kids were done.
I have her rag rugs.

Helen was strong and happy
and died too young.
I have her China—black rim
with pink flowers, still intact
half a century after her death.
Her cancer is a thread my mother
picked up. Each month
I feel for its weave.

Eleanor was thought the hardy one.
Her muscles grew taut
from hauling potatoes.
Her face grew pinched watching her sister
leave for school. As an old woman
she read romance novels
in the tub.

Eleanor and Angie wore rain bonnets
on windy days, tying the plastic tails
under their chins to protect
their short, permed hair.

They stopped going to church,
walked to the Coffee Cup
on Sunday mornings, the café thick
with cigarette smoke.

Sometimes, they loved each other dearly.
Sometimes it was all they could do
to look up from the table, their sister's face
suddenly old, and strange,
and their own.

Auction Day

All of the house and barn
were arranged on the lawn.
Preview was at 8 am.

The farmers turned rototillers on
and off and their wives
checked the pressure canners.
She kept everything
so clean, they murmured.

One table for quilts,
intimately faded
in broad daylight.

A box of half-tatted lace
you could stitch to a pillow.

The auctioneer's call wound up
then let go, like a penitent
speaking in tongues.

People talked about getting
a good deal and talked
about doing right
by the widow,

moved to the nursing home
just this past Tuesday.
Have you seen
Mrs. Slachter? they asked.

But she wasn't on hand
to witness her life
coughed up for the town
to touch.

Henry was already in the ground.

Burial

We gather near the storage shed.

Spring-in-winter, sudden thaw—it's not
the public burial (they say *you might not want
to watch*).

Cement vaults with their rows of bones
stop ground from buckling
six feet down—

and so we keep our dead from dirt,
our dirt from death. Our heels sink
into matted earth.

The grinding motor of the crane—

The concrete box, the rusted chain—

Exactly how—I cannot say—
Cement lid. Sway.

I looked away.

Underworld

Down, down to the basement,
its cool concrete kissing
our childhood feet, its rumbling
of laundry and row of cloth calendars,
one for each year starting in '74,
the basement that said *everything is redeemed.*
In the middle of summer, we hung
on the lip of the great chest freezer,
hinged at the waist to lean into its breath
so cold we coughed when it opened
like a coffin or a box that held
something we shouldn't touch, a wedding
dress, perhaps, or the suit of the uncle
who died before we were born.

Blueberry Time

We froze buckets,
and quart container
stacked on quart

marked each July,
until the assurance

of pie, bread, berries
mixed with tapioca
followed our fall.

Blueberries painted
our window-
shades before we woke.

Crisp lid removed
from each frosty box,
the next day

our fingers dripped
blue.

The Jack Loom

i.

Blue jeans torn in strips, knotted
and loomed, now rolled
before drafts or folded in closets,
faded in a kitchen
thirty years back where I sit
with Great-Grandmother playing
odd games: Kings Corner, Aggravation,
marbles ticking over the cardboard maze.
Her skin is transparent as Bible pages.
She licks one finger, flips
to another verse.

ii.

Shirts in primary colors
come in from the fields, once thick
warp and weft now a sieve.
Coveralls, curtains, housedresses
of dotted Swiss worn through Michigan
summers. We pick up the red stain
of strawberry like a ghost woven
under our feet.

iii.

Her wicker basket was a basinet
for castoffs, her scissor's mouth
measuring *waste not*
want not.

Let the treadle be similarly unrushed.
Let the weft be secure
from breast beam to back.

Let the sound of cloth
loosed into cloth
rise again
when we enter the house.

Rheum rhabarbarum (Rhubarb)

At the edge of the garden the rhubarb
grew like a sour summer sun, radiating
broad leaves above cherry red stalks.
My brother used to eat it raw
but I didn't like its sting,
preferring the bubbling
of rhubarb-raisin pies, cobblers
and crisps, the whole of Dutch baking
summed up in sugar and lard. Grandmother
said I shared her sweet tooth, as if it were
our saccharine pearl to pass down. This
is what it means to be the baby
of the family: gifted with all the odd,
calcified bits, mismatched teacups
from the tables of old ladies, tucked into
musty paper. My attic is lined
with their wishes, still waiting
for the softening, the heaped cup of sugar,
only the faintest bite
of the ground's tart kiss.

Miss Missaukee, 1966

For talent, she sang
a Cinderella song,

her hair in a kerchief,
homemade calico skirt.

Later, in mascara, another
sort of costume, her eyes

deep set wells beneath
Patty Duke hair. She hugs

the bouquet to her chest
like a child and her family

fans out around her. Proud
and stunned, sudden flash:

her mother and father,
brother, two sisters,

Grandma Alice
in horn rims and all

of my mother's trust
mooning forth in this silent,

black-and-white face.

Washing the Strawberries

They bob like red boats
in a shining sink,

well water flecked
with stray seeds.

Every sink should have
a window through which

you might watch
a cat stalk a June bug.

A few twigs rise to the surface
of the water.

In a stack nearby,
the cloudy plastic

of freezer containers waits,
opaque as heat haze.

Mother spreads tea towels
the length of the counter

and the berries bask
like swimmers

come in from the lake.
When the memory is drained,

a film of sand remains.

The Mower

Aunt Jan who was not
our aunt but a neighbor
mowed their acre
every-other day. The grass
was dry and short
as a crew cut.

She wore a tube top
that wrinkled like crepe paper
we twisted across doorways
on birthdays.

Sometimes, a grandchild
rode with her and the motor
made a bubble
where nobody spoke.

The John Deere
mapped a series of decreasing
rectangles from their pond
to the edge of our yard.

Finally, the grass
was a single strip
bringing her home
or leading away.
I don't know which
or I do.

Her dachshund
Sadie ran back and forth
on a line we called
the run.

Boat Song in F-sharp Minor

Around me, the bubble is June-light,
is silence, a cat sleeping
under the bench. At the piano
I'm floating through Mendelssohn's *Songs*,
the left hand a long-legged spider of arpeggios
moving across the bass clef.

This is the gondolier,
this is the boat—

The summer grows warm with notes
touching copper, heat rising from stones.
My friends ride by on their bright red bikes
but in the house all is a slow, measured
largo, small weight
on the metronome's highest rung,
its neck bowed
and bowing to song.

An Ordinary Sleep

I saw the spinning wheel
and wanted to play it,
wrap my arms around its spokes
like a harp.

Later, I felt
a tickle on my arm—
strand of hair
or earring fallen off.
I dreamt of houses with warped
blue shutters, ivy tentacled
across eaves.

I lay half awake
a long time. The room
close and hot. Thirsty,
thirsty. It was summer
when I slept and summer
again when I woke.

II

The Perimeter

It is wrong to suppose there was just one perimeter.
Even in the earliest days, we knew this.

A backyard with no fence, just a strange swinging gate.
Beyond that the clothesline, Mother reaching up,

wooden pins in her mouth and the air full of peonies.
Sometimes we thought of the pond as the edge,

but past that, another pond. We squatted low, stilled
while we traced the movement of tadpoles,

translucent tails slowly absorbed into body. Don't ask
of the tree. Count the strawberry garden, the cornfields'

hide-and-seek, the rows of green where we knelt
to smash potato bugs between rocks.

Don't suppose there wasn't violence from the start,
a door always slamming, small animals we trapped

and kept without feeding, peering through
aquarium walls. We recall the lilacs,

the promise of rapture. Any day. Any day.
Even the angels with their fiery swords

couldn't figure out where to stand.

Cruelty

Not like an anvil
but a sly arrow. He doled it out

slowly, stingy bites
to show we deserved nothing.

When it slept,
it kept one eye open.

When it woke, it rewrote
our history, twice, hung
its creased suits in our closets.

It explained what God thought
then gave us a wink so we'd know
it was God.

Don't get too comfortable,
it said.

When it said it loved us
it meant how unfortunate
we weren't born someone else.

Of Knowledge

Between what is dreamt and the furrows
        of waist-high pine trees

the oak's shadow rose,
        a cloud over burnt grass.

Five boards nailed into its trunk
        and a narrow plank

where the branches forked—
        Nearby, the ball diamond,

a sapling for first base where, close
        to caught, I twisted my ankle

and heard the bone crack.
        I cried out to the oak,

hard and unbending,
        which I thought meant *knowledge*

but I take it back. I hated that tree.
        Impossible to climb, bark

cutting my hands, ankle throbbing
        the next day in church

before it was wrapped
        in mummy-like strands—

my mind wild with field, the way
        I kept trying to stand.

Nobody Is Ever Missing

It was dark outside the living room
window I never knew how dark.

Mostly I saw the room mirrored back
but then movement, flicker

quick breaking the surface.
I think it's a werewolf I think

it's my brother I want to call to our
mother to let him in to keep him out

but nobody is in the room, not even me.
You need to know anything done

was done to him.
I think the window smashes.

The field went dark when we left
there were pieces that stayed.

This Other Music

Mother cans tomatoes and green beans
while I play from Bach's *Notebook*

for Anna Magdalena. The phone
rings, timer rings, cupboard doors open

and close on soft pads. Glass jars
clink into a pressure cooker

her grandmother warned
might blow through the wall,

but we're still
learning sharps and flats,

the hand held as if
lifting a bubble. The metronome

ticks, the canner ticks—
how my mother and brother

and I walk away one
hot July day, not to return

to this house where I played
on one side of the wall

and she worked on the other.
Such order and song, one hand

then the other, I don't
even realize I'm counting.

Exodus

Cleft rock.
    A woman and two children,

boy and girl,
    exit the garden on foot.

The girl's shoe falls off—now
    lopsided, now stung by thistle

and lagging—her mother
    turns back to call *hurry,*

no time to pack toothbrush
    or butterfly barrettes.

Cleft rock, fissure channeling deep
    into stone, a woman with close-

cropped hair that will soon grow out
    to a knot at her nape.

There was no snake, just
    my mother's voice, urgent,

sure as the chime
    of a church bell echoing

over the copper-tipped town.

After Blake

Blake's version of Eve:
    prayer hands slightly parted,

body arcing towards God.
    Her skin is the negative space

of the painting, a halo
    beneath the curled moon. Or

the halo emanates
    from God, his white gown

the brightest thing
    in Eden, his body a pillar

except for the arm
    that reaches, the thumb

relaxed as his palm pulls Eve up—
    And yes, the man sleeps

underneath her new feet,
    their limbs almost touching

but no sign of rib, no red gash
    in his side. She floats

like a dream or the distance
    between Adam's sleep

and God's hand, or perhaps
    God's hand measures

the distance between
            her white brow and the moon—

Blake has not made it clear,
            the hierarchy, if there is

hierarchy, but even now
            as God's hand

draws her up (or the moon
            does so), the line

of one calf suggests
            motion. Smallest flick

of Blake's wrist. Between them
            the muscle testing

its new weight forward
            into world.

The First Year

She sat at the edge of her bed,
phone tucked
between ear and shoulder.
A corkscrew line
tethered her to the wall
when the price dropped
on Sunday night.

Her grandmother said
I have broad shoulders,
you can tell me anything.

In 1988, everyone we loved
was long distance.

That year, I turned nine
and we bought a house
on a city block. I called out
to the neighbor girls across
the alley between
our upper floor rooms.

In 1988, Mother measured her grief
in twenty-cent increments.

A wire ran from the lamppost
to our house and her face was haloed
on Sunday night
as if she were speaking to that light.

Transplanting the Flowers

Four months since she walked us away
through the field, she returns
while our father's at work.
Cold rain, autumn rain,
mud slicking her jeans
as she digs up the flowers.
What she won't leave behind:
a poor woman's dowry, the perennials
separated, transplanted,
passed down.
                   Her spade
slices root. Tugs and rips
like the sound of paper tearing,
and the white thread unspooled
in her hands.

Garden Vernacular

Vernacular gardens, by definition, are gardens of ordinary people.
—Ced Dolder, "Vernacular Gardens"

Ordinary as a glass of milk, a gun,
a trio of stray cats that came to us
from the fields. Shall I name
all the flowers again? Yucca, daylily,
peony, hens-and-chicks—I'm tired of listing them.
Suffice it to say I watered those daylilies
thirty minutes each day, pulled 500 weeds
and dropped them into a Maxwell House tin,
scratched each task from my childhood
chore list as if I could answer
the world's demands.
                          When we left,
I followed the angels' decree: didn't
turn back or clap, call or croon. For a long time
I thought history went to the winners,
and we were not them.

But then our mother's new garden
unfurled, winding and strange on a city block—
the gloriosa daisies between cracks
in concrete. The ferns lapping up the dusky shade,
like *hush* and *wonder*. They tended
our secrets until our secrets no longer
needed tending.

It was not unusual to see bear cubs
in that garden. It was not unusual

to see that garden breathe.

To Find You

To find you, I go to a far
dark lane, or I go to the end
of a pier you don't know.

The last time I went back
the water was low, weeds and mud
where we once swam. The town

felt exposed. The bakery
that gave cookies for straight A's
blanched white and abandoned.

To find you now, I stay away.
I bring my brother
and we both stay away.

The drought lifts.
I splash my feet free
of sand in the plastic tub

on the stoop for this purpose,
one foot at a time, balancing.
I grow heady with the scent

of honeysuckle
and the sun-yellow paint
on the cottage, heady

as a thief, keyless and prying
the screens off the cottage windows.
Sure, the oars rest heavy

in rusty sockets—
we each struggle with one,
and mismatched once again by age,

size, and sex, we row our boat
in a slow circle. But that isn't
the worst thing, not the worst

thing at all when navigating
an island such as this.

Not Yours

That it was so overwhelmingly abandoned by everybody . . . .
It was like leaving a corpse.
   —*This American Life,* "House at Loon Lake"

Overcoats, thimbles, someone
else's newspaper clippings

turned brittle. At night, the moon
crosses the lake in ripples

like a film slowed to separate frames
but no one watches

from the screened porch. No one
takes the boat from the tangle

of grass where it rests like a tin
wishbone stalled in the night.

If you pass by a house like this
hurry on. Take your lover's hand

lightly in yours like an egg
or a piece of rotting lace.

Rosa eglanteria (Shrub Rose)

i.

Sweet briar, briar rose, brambles
      twining through wire—

The thorns reach for skin, snag shirts
      and leave shallow canals

on our arms. Summer's
      children, we shed layers

and stretch out
      our lightly furred legs, trace

the itch of mosquito, the prickling
      red line left by thorn.

ii.

Begin with a thorned list:
      raspberry, thistle, rose—

Skirt the perennial garden's artless oval,
      our mother's aim

not to arrange but to grow.
      Cotton candy, shasta daisy,

stalks scratchy as cats' tongues but
      nothing with thorns.

Only years later, moved into town,
    the roses that grew wild

behind our garage—
    tea rose or briar rose—

small and sweet-hipped with the scent
    of new apples. They coursed

over cracked paint and clung
    to the fence. She left

their small wilderness alone.
    No one would try

to pass through she said, *no one*
    could pass through that mess.

iii.

At night, she read to me of wilderness:
    Island of the Blue Dolphins,

Julie of the Wolves. On my own
    I paged through *Sleeping Beauty,*

Secret Garden. Now, trumpet vines
    loll across a fence like the wash

of their illustrations. Hedgerows
    tight as fists, music stilled

and the garden a thing stopped in time.
  And whether the wilderness lives

within or without? *Round about the castle*
  a thorn hedge began to grow,

and every year it became higher—
  Finally nothing at all could be seen of it,

not even the flag on the roof.

iv.

Everything I say is to gather
  you back. You that would not

be gathered. You that would wild
  the broken house and whip

the swings to empty tangles. You
  who sent us forth. Your name

is beyond me and yet I grow brave
  before the perimeter,

sneaking the berries golden in June
  that turn stickily ripe overnight—

then the crush in the palm,
  sudden sweet, stained, again

we turn our faces towards sun.

III

The Secret Garden Erasures

ૐ

It was "after a bit"

                and the trees
            as if   through a
long dark vault.

    The   door   massive

                the faces in the portraits
     and

      she a very small, odd little

∾

the leafless

covered a   wintry

and out of it

tendrils   made light sway

&

She remembered

crocuses   snowdrops   daffodils

the damp earth.

                              slowly

                              old border beds

                                        sharp

green

                    as if they could breathe

꙼

this new kind of creature

rather late in
remembering

the grass and
smothering

I shall come back
speaking

push   open the
door

such red   such bright   such

delighted

ह

So many places seem shut up.

I thought

I could dig somewhere

IV

Close/Close

One day, it's too much, meaning
of one thing, or *close/close,*
which can sound
like nearness (a face) one day
and another, the door
swinging shut. It takes only
the smallest latch. *When it's too much,*
she said, *I just drive.* I nod
remembering Indiana,
two-lane highways, the cliché
of cornfields made surreal
in the dark. Sixty miles south
for no reason despite
gas at over four dollars, grad school
poverty. One night, a partial
lunar eclipse. Another, almost home,
the gauge gliding to empty.
I left the car there,
the darkness cool as breath
on wet skin when I got out
and started walking.

Theme and Variations

These variations in psychological time are perceptible only as they
are related to the primary sensation—whether conscious or
unconscious—of real time, ontological time.
—Igor Stravinsky, "The Poetics of Music in Six Lessons"

Walking uphill under a parachute
of leaves rising/falling on wind

I feel the ground rise and fall.

❧

All animals have approximately
a billion and a half heartbeats,

all bodies except humans
who have learned to cheat.

❧

At the pond the frogs play slack-jawed
guitars and when they forget I am there

I forget I am there.

❧

A child's heart is the size of her fist
but an adult's heart the size of two fists.

&

Ontological time is separate
from the hummingbird's 480 beats

per minute but also from our 72.
The metronome calls this *Andante*

which means walking   which means

&

even at rest, the muscles of the heart
work hard—twice as hard

as the leg muscles of a person sprinting.

Jardins sous la pluie
          —after Debussy

The storm gathers all
          to the phrase *rustle of*—

Silks and skirts, animals tunneling
          through dense underbrush.

Rustle of curtain or sheet of paper,
          the concert program's insert

that slips to the floor. Bend down.
          Come up. On stage

the music is a pastel
          painting, left hand

hopping over the right
          as if an insect smelling rain,

then the brush against lavender
          and mint at dusk—

Dodo, l'enfant do,
          Sleep, child, sleep—

It invites the whole hand, the arms
          like lithe branches

that grow and sway,
          great tumbles of cloud-

light released from being, or
          a bell, glass on glass, the piano

again a percussive instrument,
    each bright wet dot

unrustling us from sky.

Seventy Bulbs

The tulip bulbs rest like lumps of garlic
in my hand. The allium like pearl onions
ready to grace a martini. Daffodils grow stranger,
bowing at the top like the necks of swans.
Every hole marks a dark echo in the ground.

Meanwhile the swans circle
a small circumference of pond
to keep it from freezing.

The bulbs imagine nothing but know
with uncanny precision when
the earth will be hospitable.

Origin Pantoum

I was born in the coldest month.
Clouds rustled their papers into snow.
The cat kept to herself all season,
lurking in and out of doorways.

Clouds rustled their papers and snow
covered the courthouse high on the hill.
Lurking in and out of doorways
the bell sounded its muffled hours.

In the courthouse high on the hill
secretaries took dictation like prayer.
The bell sounded its muffled hours
through the law's interior.

Secretaries took dictation like prayer
beneath diplomas on Father's walls.
Through the law's interior,
a family portrait of letters.

Beneath diplomas on Father's walls
was there a frame for my mother?
The family portrait of letters
I arrange on this page

is a frame for my mother.
Across town, snow-swept yard,
I arrange on this page
glyphs of birdseed,

invite her to the snow-swept yard.
Imagine her hand in an arc,
tossing birdseed beneath pines.
We've arrived but don't enter the home.

Imagine her hand in an arc
then the sudden pain, revelation.
We've arrived, but don't enter the home
in this version of the story.

The sudden pain, revelation,
is a message handed through halls.
In this version of the story
the meaning is outside the event,

a message handed through halls.
I was born in the coldest month,
the meaning outside the event.
The cat kept to herself all season.

Father

Even at thirty-five I can hear it,
bitter twang in my throat
like a cheap pan
I've struck with a spoon.
You were barely older
than I am today.
Does that matter? I think of you
as you are now: sitting tall
in the front pew.
Better to picture the walk
through the field,
or your skis back and forth,
the morning hours when, alone
but for the puppy brought home
when the old dog died,
you break a path
through unmarked snow.
It is not easy work. I once
followed you through it,
the slip of the skis the only
sound between us.

Conversations We Might Have Had

If you could forget about God
for a moment, I would tell you

about the birds:
three woodpeckers traveling

between the feeder and a mesh sack
filled with peanuts.

I might speak of the dog
still learning her teeth,

or the steady accumulation
of ash in the woodstove,

the flick of your wrist
as you shovel it back, automatic

gesture and everywhere
a tongue I bite, a scatter of seed

in late fall rain, this smoke
in the mouth that threatens

to spread into flame.

Virginia Regina

I always thought it was winter
that bore me. I hid
from the heat. Now I wait
on a muggy porch, still as the toad
I surprised on the sidewalk near midnight
last night, or which surprised *me*,
he never flinched, ignoring the fly
crawling over his haunch.
I thought he was dead. Then the single
blink. It's a different heat. *Virginia*, named
for the virgin queen but nothing
virginal about it. Or not as we
think it. Not as in cold, winter crackling
a spine. I remember the little piano
with that name, a rectangular box
that predated the queen,
its sides filigreed, open lid with a scene
maybe not unlike ours: painted
mountains, a path, the fields where,
we're told, there were horses
last year. Ten seconds, less,
sweat beads my hairline. Up north,
I'd go in, stand by the air conditioner
flapping my shirt. Mostly women,
today. No hoopskirts or corsets,
legs bare of the nylons
our grandmothers wore. Still,
lemonade. The verb *to sip*,
though we wish we had some bourbon and mint—
The dog lies at our feet, legs splayed

like that toad soaking up
the cool shadows. She swivels
her head to see if we've moved.
We haven't.

Slicing a Tomato

Is flesh and saturation.
The warmth
of the whetstone
or warmth of the fruit.

Hundreds in a sauce
hundreds into a canner.
Sliced over cottage cheese
and sprinkled with salt.

Eaten like an apple,
let the knife go.

All of the garden hangs
on its loud red sound.

Birding

—for my mother

Today we're out birding, you
      in your red coat, the binoculars

we borrowed swinging from our necks.
      Yellow warbler, catbird mewling.

Mostly, I'm learning to walk more slowly,
      ignore my phone's itch,

not rush you, remembering
      how we sat in a hospital room

playing cribbage while a line dripped
      into your arm, the tangle of wires

that meant I shuffled for you.
      We agreed whoever was ahead

when the doctor came in would win
      and I was relieved it was you.

You were not frightened of the knife
      but the drug that would lay you out

cold on the table—
      to disappear like that for an hour,

two, while they dug a tumor
      the size of a robin's egg

from your right breast. To not know
      where the mind will hide out,

how they'll call it back down—
        Down the hall, a woman

had both breasts removed.
        I watched her husband

in the waiting room, his eyes
        small behind tiny glasses.

They gave me a buzzer
        with flying saucer lights

that would flash when the surgery
        was over. I carried it

through labyrinth halls searching coffee,
        some off-hours café, wondered

if buying a chocolate cookie
        was wrong under the circumstances.

It took twice as long as expected.
        Twice I came to the counter

to ask if my buzzer was broken.
        When they wheeled you back swaddled

in blankets, one covering your head
        like a woozy nun, it was my turn

to fear. Couldn't find you
        anywhere in there—darting

eyes, hands like birds, your talk
        of tigers filling the room (one

just there, you pointed,
        at your side). All I could do

was say it had gone well, you
        did great, try not to look away.

Doxology

On my back
                    my ears underwater
              but not
my mouth   my breath tuned

a strange subterranean—

          I think this is what it sounds like
in my head

just air at the back of the throat
and the heart's wet thud

          I can't hear the dredge   the birds
at the fence—

Sometimes

                    it is easy to forget
parched lips   or
                         not forget

but our mouths tipping orange
                         legs drifting

the heron's world without

end/amen

The Carolina Wren

I noticed the mockingbirds first,
          not for their call but the broad white bands,

like reverse mourning bands on gunmetal
          gray, exposed during flight

then tucked into their chests.
          A thing seen once, then everywhere—

the top of the gazebo, the little cracked statue,
          along the barbed fence. Noticed because

I know first with my eyes, then followed
          their several songs braiding the trees.

Only later, this other, same-same-again song,
          a bird I could not see but heard

when I walked from the house to the studio,
          studio to the house, its three notes

repeated like a child's up and down
          on a trampoline looping

the ground to the sky—
          When I remember being a child like this

I think I wouldn't mind living alone
          on a mountain, stilled into the daily

which isn't still at all but a whirring
          gone deep. The composer shows how

the hands, palms down, thumb to thumb
　　　　and forefinger to mirrored finger, make

a shape like a cone, a honeybee hive, and then
　　　　how that cone moves across the piano—

notes in groups fluttering fast back-and-forth
　　　　and it sounds difficult but it isn't

really, how the hand likes to hover each patch
　　　　of sound. Likes *gesture*. To hold. Listening

is like this. How it took me a week to hear
　　　　the ever-there wren. And the bees

are like this, intent on their nectar,
　　　　their waggle dance better than any GPS.

A threatened thing. A no-one-knows-why.
　　　　But the wrens' invisible looping their loop—

And I, for a moment, pinned to the ground.
　　　　Pinned and spinning in the sound of it.

Perennial

We step out of a week
of thick heat. Hundreds

of hydrangeas into the cooler,
white snowball heads rising.

I want to lay my body
on the cold floor. I picture the tomb,

and then the stone rolled.
Mother plunges

into each icy bucket, comes up
with bunches of ranunculus,

phlox (I ask for each name).
Outside on their wooden stalks

finished hydrangeas dry
into flakes of gold sun.

Calendula officinalis (Marigold)

After their third daughter,
Marigold, died, the Churchills named
their next child Mary. Echo
with difference, the gold
worn off or no longer a shade
they dared name.

If I had fifty daughters
I think I'd name them all Marigold,
not nature's first green, but still gold
late in August, crinoline layers
of orange and sienna like ruffled
Flamenco hems. A strong flower,

planted near tomatoes
to protect against pests—
when I snip finished blooms,
the stalks breathe a peppery scent.

What I Still Will Not Ask

Now it seems the window has closed
when I might have asked,
"When did it start?" Meaning
"had you chosen her before we left?"
A braver daughter might ask, but I know
it matters less than it seems
and know, too, the answer,
the choice long before. Weeks
or years, how he talked of her
and her bright daughters
at the table and our mother said,
"I wish you'd stop talking of them,"
my brother and I sitting there,
two young lumps, not
knowing how to wear the shine
of that family, not yet
knowing if we should try.
And again, I'm failing to ask him his side.
In the weeks after we left,
her daughters' photos populated
our old fridge. Across one wall, drawings
these other girls made
of the cats, *my* cats, Whiskers
and Puffy, Midnight,
George and Tyg. Back for "visitation"
I crawled under a desk,
hugged Puffy to my chest—
he'd been born in my closet,
my mother there helping
the tired mother cat with this last
of her litter. The first six,
matched pairs, then this runt.
Of course we'd kept him,

even after his minutes-older
siblings were gone.
And then he, too, was gone. Father,
I mean it as kindness, not asking,
not making you say what we know.
My silence—once shame, now meant
as the only forgiveness I own. It is clear
how much more sense they make
as your daughters, and Faye
by your side (though you might
have tried?)—

                  how little
it matters when it all began. How
ridiculous a question—both of you
in your seventies, her hearing
strained. Today I worry more
about who will die first. I picture you
left at loose ends in old age.
I do not wish this for you.
Whatever bitterness
you still hear in my voice,
it pains me to imagine you alone.
How much better suited
Mother was for it. After that first, terrible
plunge, decades to learn
how to swim to the other side
of the self and back.

Eden through Milk Eyes

I almost bought
    an antique lightning rod

for its milk glass bauble
    on tarnished copper,

strung like a bead
    the size of a softball.

The owner explains how
    most filled with rain-

water, froze and cracked,
    but this one still intact—

he probably just wants
    a better price. *It's*

lovely, I say, picturing
    different eyes, opaque

but with the lure
    of translucence, thinking

if I turned the globe just right
    I too might see

straight through.

The Last Supper

Great-Aunt Gert spreads the table
with thick, sliced tomatoes, mashed potatoes
and gravy, meatballs, white bread,

corn on the cob she picked from the garden
we passed when we turned up the driveway.
An angel food cake rests in its round tin.

My boys take care of me, says Aunt Gert,
who lives alone at ninety-one. At eighteen,
she married Grandpa Philip's brother,

don't ever live with your in-laws! she laughs,
glancing towards the ceiling, the room upstairs
where she and Otto and the baby all slept.

She'll be dead in six months, but today
she is sharper than either of us.
We've come for an old woman's stories

and she has been waiting—
she tells how the barn collapsed like a lung,
the milking tanks lost beneath shingles.

It wasn't the lightning but wind
that took it. *I'm sorry,*
she says, *should have warned you on the phone*

*before you came. But remember that storm
in the fifties? The whole herd struck,
current bouncing between.* Somewhere,

a newspaper clipping. *Remember,*
remember she urges my mother—
when Grandpa Toby ran off the banker

with a pitchfork? And that preacher
who treated his family so bad?
The whole town knew. She stares hard

at my mother. We don't talk
of Uncle Otto's affair.
We don't talk of how my mother

fled this place. We know.
We know. And the knowing swells
like the chainsaw song of cicadas

buzzing through heat, it grows large
around the milk jug on the table
and the TV left droning

from the next room. It grows large
as summer unzipped from the earth,
how it won't be contained. It fills

and takes. *Soon,* Aunt Gert says,
but I am not afraid. She sighs herself
up from the long kitchen table.

She will not let us leave empty.

Summer

I was wrong to divide us
        into inside and out.

Thunder rolling but still
        more to say. A single

kind person can break me
        open. One mountain

covered in rain, one not,
        but between them

no line. It was all garden
        and it was all not.

My Life had stood a poem
        that could and could not

hold two worlds at once.
        The middle of summer

is always like this, why
        I have only ever

fallen in love in summer.
        A single kind gesture.

The longest day
        spinning close

and then closer.
        Stormshine, heat,

release from.

Notes on the Poems

"Charlotte Sometimes" is titled after the children's book by Penelope Farmer.

"Elsie and Florence": The epigraph is from an unpublished account my great-grandmother, Alice Slachter, wrote of her childhood in Northern Michigan.

"Inheritance" is after Kathleen Norris's poem "A Poem about Faith."

"After Blake" is inspired by Blake's illustration *The Creation of Eve*, part of his 1808 series of scenes from *Paradise Lost*.

"Nobody Is Ever Missing" takes its title from Berryman's "Dream Song 29."

"Rosa eglanteria (Shrub Rose)*"* quotes the Grimm Brothers' fairytale "Briar Rose" in the italicized lines at the end of the poem's third section.

"The Secret Garden Erasures": Each erasure takes its text from a single page of Frances Hodgson Burnett's *The Secret Garden* (HarperCollins, 1985 edition). The spacing of the original text is roughly preserved.

"Theme and Variations": Most of this poem's facts about the heart are found at *Nova Online,* "Amazing Heart Facts." The italicized lines are direct quotations from this site.

"Jardins sous la pluie" (*"Gardens in the Rain"*) is titled after the third movement of Claude Debussy's piano piece *Estampes* (*Prints*).

"Virginia Regina" and "The Carolina Wren" are dedicated to the Virginia Center for Creative Arts.

"Calendula officinalis (Marigold)*"* quotes Robert Frost's "Nothing Gold Can Stay."

"Summer" quotes Emily Dickinson's "My Life had stood—a Loaded Gun—" and is indebted to Marianne Boruch for the final line's cadence.

Thank You

A million thanks to Maggie Smith for selecting this manuscript and to her, Jack Ridl, and Jessica Jacobs for sending it into the world with their words. Thank you to Paige Webb, Deborah Fleming, Jennifer Rathbun and Ashland Poetry Press for making this book a reality. Thank you to Debora Greger and the Abbot and Holder Gallery for the cover art *After Eden, Eve, I* and to Nicholas Fedorchak for designing the cover.

Thank you to the Virginia Center for the Creative Arts, the Sewanee Writers' Conference, and the I-Park Foundation for fellowships providing time, inspiration, and camaraderie. Thank you to the State University of New York at Oswego for travel grants supporting this work.

Thank you to poetry mentors and friends: Priscilla Atkins, Katherine Bode-Lang, Elizabeth Lyons, Jennifer K. Sweeney, Donna Steiner, Jack Ridl, Joan Conway, Marianne Boruch, Nancy Eimers, Mark Jarman, Joan Houlihan, Greg Williamson, and all the members of the Sewanee and Colrain poetry workshops. You have made this book (and my life) better. Thank you for support, inspiration, and friendship: Megan Donnelly, Christine Haskill, Rebekah Silverman, Andrew Bode-Lang, Sarah Yaw, Leigh Wilson, Allison Rank, Mary Bartok, the Soiree Sisters, the PACT crew, the River's End Bookstore, and my colleagues and students at SUNY Oswego.

Thank you to my aunts and uncles—Lois and Karl Schripsema and Virginia and Steve Oakley—for giving us a safe place to land when we needed it. To my grandfather Clifford Quist, gone too soon but with me in the garden. Thank you to the Luidens family for love along the way. And to Beth and Roger Kolp, and Elizabeth, Ashley, Alex, and Ava John for kindness, generosity, and laughter. I'm so grateful to be part of your family.

Thank you to the grandmothers, great-aunts, and great-grandmothers, especially to my mother's mother, Angeline Quist, and to her mother, Alice Slachter. I stand on the shoulders of giants.

To my brother, John Donnelly, there from the start, first teacher, first friend. Thank you for the postcards. Thank you, so much, for supporting this book.

Thank you to Benjamin Kolp for unwavering support, love, and humor. And to Sue, the best work buddy. You two are my team.

Thank you to my mother, Karen Alice Donnelly, for making the impossible decision and for teaching me how to find grace in the garden. There is no one kinder or stronger.

Thank you to the garden and the lake.

To anyone finding their way out, their way back, this book is for you.

The Richard Snyder Publication Series

This book is the 20th in a series honoring the memory of Richard Snyder (1925–1986), poet, fiction writer, playwright and longtime professor of English at Ashland University. Snyder served for fifteen years as English Department chair and was co-founder (in 1969) and co-editor of the Ashland Poetry Press. He was also co-founder of the Creative Writing major at the school, one of the first on the undergraduate level in the country. In selecting the manuscript for this book, the editors kept in mind Snyder's tenacious dedication to craftsmanship and thematic integrity.

Deborah Fleming, Editor and Director, selected finalists for the 2019 contest. Final judge: Maggie Smith

Snyder Award Winners:

> 1997: Wendy Battin for *Little Apocalypse*
> 1998: David Ray for *Demons in the Diner*
> 1999: Philip Brady for *Weal*
> 2000: Jan Lee Ande for *Instructions for Walking on Water*
> 2001: Corrinne Clegg Hales for *Separate Escapes*
> 2002: Carol Barrett for *Calling in the Bones*
> 2003: Vern Rutsala for *The Moment's Equation*
> 2004: Christine Gelineau for *Remorseless Loyalty*
> 2005: Benjamin S. Grossberg for *Underwater Lengths in a Single Breath*
> 2006: Lorna Knowles Blake for *Permanent Address*
> 2007: Helen Pruitt Wallace for *Shimming the Glass House*
> 2008: Marc J. Sheehan for *Vengeful Hymns*
> 2009: Jason Schneiderman for *Striking Surface*
> 2010: Mary Makofske for *Traction*
> 2011: Gabriel Spera for *The Rigid Body*
> 2012: Robin Davidson for *Luminous Other*
> 2013: J. David Cummings for *Tancho*
> 2014: Anna George Meek for *The Genome Rhapsodies*
> 2015: Daneen Wardrop for *Life As* It
> 2016: Pamela Sutton for *Burning My Birth Certificate*
> 2017: Michael Moos for *Idea of the Garden*
> 2018: Barbara Ungar for *Save Our Ship*
> 2019: Laura Donnelly for *Midwest Gothic*